The Right Moves
A Collection of Strategies for Business
Volume 1

by

Ann Chadwell Humphries

of

ETICON, Inc.
Etiquette Consultants for Business
P.O. Box 290116
Columbia, South Carolina 29229

Edited by
Helen James Hutson

Dedication:

*To all those people who
said they were proud of me.*

Foreword

by Fred Monk
Business Editor at The State

In today's complex world of business, people often overlook that a simple action can make a difference.

Ann Chadwell Humphries has been imparting simple but sound advice on how to act your best in the workplace, in business meetings, at social events, and even in those awkward spontaneous situations we all find ourselves in through her business etiquette column, "The Right Moves."

"The Right Moves" has been a fixture in *The State*, South Carolina's largest newspaper, for over two years. Another 250 newspapers have had access to her down-to-earth advice through the Knight Ridder News service.

Her columns on everything from table manners to forgetting people's names have generated considerable mail from enthusiastic readers, not only in the United States, but from foreign countries as well. As a result, she has been asked to make personal presentations based on the columns she has written for *The State*. And she has been interviewed by media across the country on stories involving etiquette in business situations.

What makes Ann Humphries' column so popular? She tells it straight. She doesn't beat around the bush. She presents herself clearly. She uses real-life situations. But most importantly, she has news you can use — like how much to eat at the next reception you attend, how to politely not overindulge, or the ramifications of the clothes you wear, such as the low cut dress at the holiday party.

Good manners and proper etiquette aren't faddish, they are essential for anyone who wants to make his or her best presentation, get the best results out of their time and effort, and establish relationships that are enjoyable and meaningful — whether you're a salesperson or a CEO.

The way you act is one of the strongest communications signals you send, sometimes without saying a word. Your actions describe your interpersonal skills and a sense of caring. Bottom line, it can make or break your rise in a company or that multi-million dollar contract, not to mention getting along with those around you.

Ann's columns aren't hard to read and provide basic information that people sometimes have difficulty learning, if not mastering.

Have fun thumbing through Ann's columns. You'll dog-ear a number of them, and you'll also think twice about the next plate of boiled shrimp you chow down on at the business reception — no matter how good it tastes.

Introduction

By Ann Chadwell Humphries

Think about the people in your life who have exceptional manners. I bet you can name them and the characteristics you admire about them. They are probably successful in their professional and personal lives. They aren't free of problems, but you admire how they are able to resolve delicate issues and complicated situations. You respect, even revere these individuals.

Think, too, of the people in business who have poor manners, who don't succeed as well as they could because they are limited in their ability to treat others with respect. Either they don't know any better, or worse, they think they can get away with it.

Because your ability to communicate with others is crucial to your professional life, this booklet is designed to give you quick and practical instructions to daily business etiquette dilemmas. It's time important questions were answered.

"Why etiquette in business?"

In today's business world, astute business professionals, like yourself, recognize the value of mastering etiquette skills. You know you must produce or manage production in a sophisticated, increasingly service-oriented business culture. And that culture is not only occupied with demanding and diverse clients, but also with talented coworkers, colleagues, superiors, subordinates, and unrelenting competition.

As a business professional, you want value in your work and in your life. Etiquette complements your training, your service, product, or whatever it is you must achieve or do in your professional life. It helps you become more polished, confident, and self-assured. It checks arrogance and helps you develop judgment to understand what is important and what is not. In business today, etiquette is not only respected, it is expected.

"Why has it been so difficult to find information?"

Simply put, there has been little training. While most etiquette books have provided guidance, it has been for life in general, drawing little distinction between protocol for business and social situations. Busy, working people want easily referenced, user-friendly sources for problems they face in their work. That's why I began my business and how this column evolved — to support business professionals who want information about issues in their professional lives and want it presented in a direct manner.

"Why is interest in business etiquette increasing?"

• International workplace

One reason people are focusing on business etiquette corresponds directly to the emerging international workplace. More and more, we are working with people from different cultures and countries. By observing business practices from around the world, we gain perspective about our American style of business and often find that it is more informal than other cultures. In order to compete globally, we need to pay attention to international etiquette. By seeing ourselves as others see us, we can work more sensitively and more effectively abroad and at home.

• Women in the workplace

Social etiquette traditionally defers to women because they are women. In business, these customs are not only unnecessary, they can also be offensive. In today's work environment, authority and position are to be honored first, regardless of gender. Distinguishing between social and business etiquette can be confusing for both men and women. Yet this knowledge is vital to succeed in business.

• Quality of life

Another reason for interest in etiquette is the general trend toward value and quality of life. We spend a great amount of time at work, so we want that time to be spent on meaningful work with people we enjoy. Awareness of etiquette enables people to get along better, makes the workplace an easier place to be productive in, and adds pleasure and satisfaction to life. You learn how to treat others and yourself respectfully and courteously.

"What can etiquette do for me?"

There is much etiquette can do for you. It will help you work with diverse groups of people, create options for what to do when you forget someone's name, make you comfortable in a variety of settings, empower and distinguish you. As you read this booklet, you will understand just how helpful etiquette can be.

But before you begin scanning these columns for information for your particular needs, you should know what etiquette won't do for you. It won't allow you to stand in judgment of others who are less refined or rougher around the edges than you think they should be, for their generosity and character may surprise you.

Etiquette is intolerant of being too "process-oriented," too focused on rigidity, or obsessed with doing things properly. In other words, etiquette does not complement elitism or inflexibility.

It won't help you be "nice" all the time, for no one likes superficial friendliness. You *will* encounter difficult and unpleasant situations. You *will* have to make difficult choices. You *will* have to deliver bad news. But etiquette will give you the tools to handle these situations with grace.

And knowing etiquette will not make your sense of humor or sense of fun disappear. You will still be able to laugh long and loud, slap your knees, and play good-natured pranks on your friends.

I'm hopeful you will find this book convenient and helpful for your professional life.

P.S. I'm always interested in a good (or bad) story on manners. Call us if you have one or if there is an issue that you would like us to address.

Table of Contents

Telephone Etiquette

Business Meeting and Presentation Skills

Sales Etiquette

Your Business Appearance

Business Social Events

Job Search Skills

International Business Etiquette

Etiquette Increases Business And Professional Success

Etiquette provides exceptional benefits to your business and professional life, benefits and advantages necessary to compete in the 1990's.

The hierarchic pyramid based on command and control is no longer effective. For too long, business people have been able to be rude to one another in the name of speed, the "bottom line," productivity, and a plentiful supply of workers. As a result, these patterns have created a work force that is less loyal to the organization and more mobile and individualistic.

However, people are now labeling inappropriate business behavior for what it is — blunt, abrupt, untrustworthy— and are holding others to higher standards of conduct. Fed up with bellicose demands that benefit only the company, workers now expect dignity and involvement.

According to business trend predictors, future organizations will become flatter with fewer management levels and fewer chances for formal promotion. The roles of teams will

1

Etiquette provides solutions for how to react to unpredictable, high-pressure situations. It gives you the flexibility you will need to move in and out of different teams, and in and among the various companies and diverse groups you may work with.

grow, requiring workers to be responsible, informed, and contributing team members able to work productively with peers.

In today's business world, etiquette makes you more competitive. It increases your options, both in knowing how to manage people and how to present yourself in the most appealing way.

It provides solutions for how to react to unpredictable, high-pressure situations. It gives you the flexibility you will need to move in and out of different teams and in and among the various companies and diverse groups you may work with. It helps you understand ethical components of the workplace and creates a value system that builds personal integrity and earns respect.

And as an employer, knowing the principles of etiquette will enable you to recruit, retain, and motivate your workers more effectively, as well as increase your sensitivity and responsiveness to customers.

Good Manners Foster Good Business

Do these situations sound familiar?

Scenario One: Your staff does its job well, but when it comes to working with customers, your workers need polish.

Scenario Two: You receive your well-deserved promotion. Now you are more visible and face situations which require not only your technical ability, but diplomacy and social savvy. You could use a brush up on how to respond in certain situations.

The way you do business is as important as the business you do. Nationally, there is a surging interest in business etiquette. Business and industry see that good manners are part of working smart.

Rudeness, whether intended or not, is bad business. And individuals now recognize the value of basic social skills to further their careers.

The benefits are numerous:

• Etiquette fosters business by building credibility and establishing rapport quickly.

***The way you do business is as
important as the business you do.***

- It protects valuable business investments in sensitive work situations.
- It smooths the business process in a workplace that is more diverse and global than ever before.

Today, seminars in business etiquette include: the strategy of business social events — from breakfast and lunch meetings to cocktail parties; mastering introductions and small talk; proper etiquette at meetings; telephone styles; personal business correspondence; your business appearance; the art of giving and receiving compliments, criticisms, and apologies; surviving and thriving company mergers and reorganizations; human relations in the workplace; and business travel.

Etiquette encompasses aspects of economic development that can bolster a community's ability to compete for jobs.

Whether you call it etiquette or just good manners, common courtesy is capturing the attention of people in today's workplace.

Etiquette Promotes Professional Conduct

Etiquette offers many benefits for business. It improves relationships with clients and coworkers. It creates options for handling difficult situations. It boosts confidence and lends professional credibility to individuals in the workplace.

To prepare for the 90s, here is a short list of characteristics of professionals with impeccable manners. Imagine how these qualities can improve your ability to conduct your business well.

True professionals:

• Respect the time of others. They are punctual in attending business meetings and honoring deadlines. If they must be late, they let people know ahead of time and apologize for any inconveniences.

• Are sensitive about interrupting the work and thoughts of

Show respect to others regardless of their position or background.

others.

• Are careful about how they express themselves in the words they select, the tone of voice they use, and the manner in which they speak.

• Are consistent in their demeanor and not given to wordiness, sulking, or intimidation.

• Know what behaviors are expected for special occasions.

• Show respect to others by addressing and listening to them, regardless of their position or background.

• Comply with the rules that apply to everyone and don't press for exceptions for themselves.

• Challenge unfair policies.

• Allow people to save face when appropriate.

Do The Common Things Uncommonly Well

Astute business professionals are ever vigilant to techniques to enhance their ability to do well. Their deliberate, disciplined search is turning more and more to etiquette. Recent articles in *Fortune, Barrons' Business Weekly*, and *The Wall Street Journal* have documented the interest of corporate America in etiquette as a strategy for business.

One of the basic maxims of etiquette relevant to business is: "Do the common things uncommonly well." Greeting guests and newcomers is one of the areas which makes a profound impact upon others either by its conspicuous absence or presence.

Bob Heffron, president of Heffron, Ingle, McDowell and Cooper insurance agency, and former president of Charleston's Trident Chamber of Commerce, knows the business value of making people feel comfortable and showing them basic common courtesies.

He says, "Because we are a service business and sell an intangible product, we must communicate a sense of caring and responsiveness to our customers. The way we greet people, even our buildings and furnishings, is specifically designed to communicate a sense of caring, responsiveness, and success." Heffron sees and applies the benefits of etiquette to his business.

The following are common courtesies that will also benefit you:

"The way we greet people, even our buildings and furnishings, is specifically designed to communicate a sense of caring, responsiveness and success."

• Consider who might be a guest or a newcomer. Examples include recent appointees to standing committees, clients seeking entitled benefits, new members of associations, prospective employees, newly elected board members, or perhaps even neighbors who have moved from out of town.

• Evaluate how your organization greets newcomers or guests. Is your closest parking assigned to visitors or prominently marked, "Reserved for staff"? Do your receptionists look up and smile when someone arrives at their desk? Are chairs available, current reading material, access to refreshments, even a telephone?

• Introduce yourself to newcomers and guests and see that they are introduced to others. How many meetings have you been asked to join and only the chairman knows everybody? Clarify the roles of guest and host.

Communicating a genuine spirit of welcome in the business world can protect your business investments, in how you retain your staff, how productive your committees are, how trusting your clients are of you, even in recruiting industry to your community.

It's the common oversights that undermine business relationships. Let your uncommon perception and communication skills help create a caring and spirited work environment.

Handbook Untangles Common Etiquette Knots

Business professionals today excel in so many areas, but the pesky little common courtesies — how to handle long lines, elevators, doors, coats, and packages — give us all fits. Men can feel silly for letting dozens of women go first, only to get rebuked with "I can do it myself, thank you." And people consistently cause major traffic jams when they open doors, exit elevators, or descend an aisle.

Esquire magazine has published an entertaining etiquette handbook, *Esquire Etiquette,* which helps sort out these every-day dilemmas with humor and common sense.

It prefaces its "Streetwalking" chapter with "The essence of good form in changing times is that you follow the rules of behavior that make sense and replace the ones that don't. Sometimes, you hang on to a habit just because it still feels right." Here are summary tips for everyday life:

• Elevators — Help with the door. Let people off before you get in. Last one on, first one off, then, step aside.

• Doors — Generally, in business, whomever gets there first opens it. No need for men to rush ahead or for women to slow

"The essence of good form in changing times is that you follow the rules of behavior that make sense and replace the ones that don't."

down. Although traditionally women go first, be gracious and don't cause a scene.

• Coats and packages—Offer first, then people can either accept or decline.

• Walking—Although the reason is obsolete – to protect women from mud-splashing horses – men customarily walk on the street side of women. It's one of those rules to retain, because it seems to work. At other times, women walk to the man's right. How to remember? "Woman" has the same number of letters as "right."

• Lines—Avoid cutting in lines and don't dart in front of people. If two of you reach a narrow pass, defer to the older person, or if the same age, the woman. And be especially considerate, not patronizing, to handicapped people, pregnant women, or those with small children. Remember, offer first.

Handling these everyday common courtesies makes life simpler and easier. Pick your battles and be considerate of each other.

A Quick Greeting May Lead To Better Business

One of the most common courtesies I notice that set the stage for respect, recognition, and productivity is extending a simple, quick greeting to people before conducting business.

Whether standing at the counter ordering, passing in the hallways, or beginning a meeting, acknowledging those present with a nod, a smile, or an introduction opens the floor for business in a manner that is friendly and productive.

Three times recently, I have noticed the power of this simple gesture. I used to share an office suite with the Rev. David Landholt, chairman of South Carolina's Board of Social Services.

While most people around the office rushed in and prepared for the intensity of the day, David would work his way to his office greeting people, not in a way that called attention to himself, but because he was genuinely interested in opening relationships, not just the doors for business.

"Around here, we start business with a 'Hello' first."

During a United Way presentation, Miriam Evans, executive director of Alston Wilkes youth home, told the audience one of the basic skills she coaches the young men on is letting the staff know when they would be coming or going. This communication was important because many of the young men came from homes where no one cared if they were there or not.

One final example concerns a man who rented mopeds at a vacation spot. When a customer barked across the room, "Hey, is this where you rent bikes?" he responded with, "Around here, we start business with a 'Hello' first."

Look for opportunities to greet people, even tell them goodbye. Make them feel a part of the organization, that they have a place, and that they are noticed when they are missing. You will reap obvious dividends of accountability and loyalty.

Introductions Open Doors To Opportunity

One of the hallmarks of self-assured business professionals, and those destined to succeed, is the ability to introduce themselves easily.

Whether at a professional meeting, the inevitable cocktail party, or company water cooler, people who easily meet others have developed a valuable business tool. This makes them a tribute to their company and sets them apart from their peers.

Here are techniques to meet people easily:

• Initiate your own introductions. According to Pat Smith, vice president of purchasing and regulatory affairs with South Carolina Electric & Gas Co., "Even people with household names introduce themselves. People have trouble remembering names on the spot. By introducing yourself, you take people off the spot, and they appreciate that."

In many social settings, business professionals hover in the corner or only talk to people they know. Employees mull over whether they should speak to the company vice president. Walk up to people and tell them who you are.

• Prepare a five-second commercial for yourself. In today's world of quick media messages, people make instant judgments

"By introducing yourself, you take people off the spot, and they appreciate that."

on whether they want more information about you. Work to project confidence and competence quickly.

Although occasions vary, decide what you want people to know about you, then project it in positive terms — you are good at your work, you are proud of your company. Work to create the message that you have a future.

• Rehearse. It won't sound stilted. It will sound poised and in control. Watch for the people who murmur. They don't seem as effective.

• Say your name lower and slower. Give people a chance to hear your name. People will pay attention, and you will be remembered.

• Say what you do in plain English. Help people understand what you do. Your audience will glaze over if you recite heavy technical titles. Give people a brief, light description of your work.

As Ms. Smith affirms, "Manners make people feel good, and in business, when you make people feel good, you have helped yourself immeasurably."

It's Not All In The Name When Introductions Become Awkward

One of the most awkward, yet common, etiquette dilemmas is forgetting someone's name.

Here are straightforward strategies to help you through what need not be an embarrassing situation.

• Consider that it is not always your fault. You may not recognize people for good reasons. People change their appearance. They may be out of context with how you know them. And people don't always introduce themselves in a manner to be remembered. They slur their words, race through their names, or present themselves in an indistinct way that is easy to forget. Stop feeling guilty.

• When you can, introduce yourself. Anticipate not only when you might not remember someone, but when they might not remember you. Your initiative takes you both off the spot. And when someone introduces themselves to you, don't say, "Of course I know you!" Say your name back to them.

• Introduce the people you know. As you go around the group, pause when you get to the person's name you have

"I'm so sorry. I know who you are, but I've drawn a blank."

forgotten. A gracious person will fill in the blank and introduce themselves.

• Stall for time and concentrate. Ever feel yourself withdrawing from or avoiding those you don't know? Ever see someone sport a silly, nervous smile while they work to remember, "Who IS this?"

Just relax and pay attention. Act as if you know them. Be friendly. A clue may surface. Focus on them, not on yourself.

• If you are forced to introduce someone, say with a "silly me" manner, "I'm so sorry. I know who you are, but I've drawn a blank," and laugh it off.

• Don't go to people and say, "Remember me?" And don't get upset if people forget your name, unless, of course, they do it repeatedly.

Forgetting names happens to everyone, and memory lapses occur at the most inopportune times. But people don't judge you on singular events. Rather, they judge you on how you handle awkward situations and how you operate over time.

When You Meet An Officeholder, You Are Also Meeting A Titleholder

A friend you've known for years has been elected to office. A judge has joined your church. You find yourself visiting with a former legislator while your children play soccer.

What do you call these people in social conversations? How do you address correspondence to them?

These questions send us scurrying to the etiquette books to check how we should address public officials, for we know the importance of properly addressing people, especially in correspondence and conversation.

No one wants to embarrass themselves by overkill or disrespect, but finding help is difficult.

Etiquette books differ on the subject. Although they present protocol for top public officials and foreign diplomats, we also need to know how to address officeholders on the state and local level — the ones we're more likely to meet.

Here are a few tips to keep in the back of your mind as you circulate with elected officials:

• A person who holds or has held high office at the federal or state level holds the title "The Honorable" for life, unless he

We need to know how to address office-holders on the state and local level — the ones we're more likely to meet.

or she has left office in disgrace or under question. Use this when you address correspondence or introduce governors, lieutenant governors, state and U.S. senators and representatives, and judges.

As for officeholders at county and city levels, Howard Duvall, director of intergovernmental relations of the Municipal Association of South Carolina, says, "The custom is to use 'The Honorable' for individuals who currently hold office. Once their terms are over, they revert back to 'Mr.' or 'Ms.' The exception is to use the honorific for a former mayor who held the office a long time."

• Once a senator, always a senator. Use this title whether they are a standing or former officeholder. The same rule applies for presidents, governors, lieutenant governors, and judges at the state and U.S. level. Representatives are properly addressed as "Mr. Smith" or "Ms. Jones," but are customarily called "Representative," "Congressman," or "Congresswoman."

Coping With Inevitable Conflicts Is The Mark Of A Polished Professional

Among the skills of a polished business professional is knowing how to handle conflict.

Thinking the workplace will be conflict free is naive and unrealistic, for conflict is a part of living, a part of working.

Here are basic strategies for managing conflict and confrontation and for how to disagree diplomatically:

• Decide if it's worth it. Many times, we can lose perspective about how important issues may or may not be in the workplace.

Ask yourself: Is this a real problem? Do I deny this is important? Will time solve this?

Denials may force issues underground where they build and emerge with more power and venom. You will want to act if a conflict is pesky and persistent. Or you may choose to allow "heat-of-the-moment" issues to cool first.

• Honor your opponent. Remember, you may not like them

Work to fix the problem, not affix blame.

personally, but you can honor their position. Try to see things from their perspective. What drives them on this point? What might be preventing a solution — deadlines, money, staff?

By respecting your opponent, you may avoid entrenched positions defended on the basis of pride and principle.

• Work to fix the problem, not affix blame. Slice conflict into manageable pieces. Be as specific as possible. Assess where there is agreement, where you can give. Have backup strategies. And don't overlook easy solutions.

• Choose time and place carefully. Few people enjoy being surprised or embarrassed. Consider methods of how you can allow your opponents to retain their options and dignity.

Conflict is inevitable. At times, you must force it. It usually is not pleasant, but mastering strategies for dealing with conflict well will win you a reputation that is admired and respected.

Acknowledging Mistakes And Apologizing Show Courage

As I skimmed the summaries of graduation messages, one by former Citadel President James Grimsley to the military college's cadet corps stopped me.

Among many challenges, Grimsley advised: "If you have blown it, have the moral courage to say so. Then, have the fiber and pride to correct your mistakes and grow from your experience."

There is so much talk from the business world that encourages us to be risk-takers and to not be afraid to make mistakes in our quest for excellence. What I don't see, however, is much information encouraging us to take responsibility for our mistakes or to admit error.

Many of the business people I speak with find it difficult to apologize. One told me recently that apologies catch in his throat. Another told me of never hearing a spouse say, "I'm sorry."

Granted, some people are harder to apologize to than others. But more often, an apology is difficult and generally avoided because it calls attention to mistakes. And consistent

There is so much talk from the business world that encourages us to be risk-takers and to not be afraid to make mistakes in our quest for excellence. What I don't see, however, is much information encouraging us to take responsibility for our mistakes or to admit error.

mistakes are not long tolerated in business.

Yet, mastering the skills of admitting error and apologizing can help you in your business life. Here are just a few techniques to make your apologies more effective:

• Acknowledge results of errors. "Gee, I didn't mean it," does not serve as an apology. Anyone can say that. Nor does giving reasons for your action. As a good friend says, "That may be the reason, but that is no excuse."

• Consider action to assuage. If you have erred and apologized, say for a late shipping, you can sweeten the package by sending something extra, something to build goodwill.

• And finally, decide what you need to apologize for and what you shouldn't. If it is your job to take an action that offends or upsets people, take the responsibility. You can acknowledge people's feelings: "I'm sorry this has upset you," or "I regret this happened." Guard against pity.

I agree with President Grimsley. Acknowledging mistakes and apologizing take moral courage, but they also reveal it.

Responding Properly To Criticism Is A Good Way To Boost A Career

"People take criticism so personally that it is difficult to give it without people overreacting," a supervisor recently confided. "Please tell employees to understand this is part of business and not a personal affront."

Whether about your individual performance or the performance of your service, criticism is difficult to receive. But if you are able to accept it professionally, you will uncover a source of insight and strength that can boost your career.

Cathy Dabeck, director of Trenholm Road United Methodist Church Preschool, incorporates professional etiquette guidelines that enable her to understand criticism and respond to it appropriately. Here are techniques that will help you:

• Listen to what the criticism is. Be open to hear it out. "Withhold judgment about the person and what they are saying," Ms. Dabeck said.

• Express genuine concern for the comment. Show respect for the other person by saying, "I am so glad you told me," or "I appreciate your input," or "Thanks for taking the time to let me know." Recognizing that you are not always right indicates

"Thanks for taking the time to let me know."

maturity, an open mind, and willingness to change.

That is much better than sulking or reacting sourly to company policy or denying bad news. Try to see things from the criticizer's perspective.

• Understand the emotion behind the criticism. "I can see how you feel that way," and "I understand," can help people feel they have been heard.

Even if criticism is inappropriately given, Ms. Dabeck said, "Make a decision not to become emotional or argumentative. Just get through it. Sit down later and analyze what was said. If true, apologize and correct. If untrue, follow-up and defend without being defensive.

"Excuses don't work," Ms. Dabeck said. "Reasons for error are not what people want to hear." And it sounds argumentative, which is not good business practice.

Expect criticism. Part of wisdom in business comes from acknowledging, not overlooking, mistakes, correcting them when they occur, and being willing to change when necessary.

Well-Placed Compliments Are An Effective Management Tool

Recognition for work well done is a basic human need. Employees tell me over and over, "If the boss would just say something kind," or "The only recognition I receive is when I screw up."

Even supervisors acknowledge they often operate on the "No news is good news theory," or "I'll be darned if I'm going to compliment them on something that is an expected part of their job."

Inc. magazine reported a survey of what motivates managers: 91 percent of the respondents repeated "recognition for a job well done." It was third highest after "challenging work" and "my opinion matters." No big surprise. What is surprising is that only 55 percent of the respondents said that recognition existed in their workplace.

We all know the value of recognizing good works, of catching people doing things right, or celebrating accomplishments. Yet knowing what to do and actually doing it are often far out of balance.

Here is a review of the basics of recognition, specifically giving compliments, so that you acknowledge the good work

"The only recognition I receive is when I screw up ."

done by your employees and motivate them to do even better.

• Deliver the compliment to the scale of the event. If you are complimenting a small action, be brief, direct, and move on. Don't gush. In contrast, don't send a form memo to your committee who worked overtime and personally sacrificed to complete a major project. Celebrate. Have dinner or take a day of rest.

And keep regular awards ceremonies interesting and important. Often these become ho-hum and lack the participation of top management. Be imaginative so people understand that you appreciate them.

• Isolate your compliments. Let them stand alone. I find managers undermine the effectiveness of recognition by sandwiching compliments with criticism.

• Consider the purpose of your compliment. If it is to call attention to yourself, then you are only complimenting your own self-righteousness.

A genuine and sincere compliment honors and recognizes others.

Compliments Should Be Given With Sincerity

Ever have a coworker or boss overcompliment work you considered an expected part of your job? Ever receive a standard form letter for a project that required professional and personal sacrifice?

The art of giving compliments — and receiving them — is the mark of a confident, effective business person. This skill can be refined into a valuable business asset by reviewing basic etiquette guidelines.

• Keep compliments to the scale of the action. People who gush about ordinary things loose their credibility quickly. We question their sincerity and their wisdom to judge what is important.

On the other hand, people who either withhold compliments or standardize praise jeopardize the trust of others. Overcomplimenting and undercomplimenting raise an issue of judgment and appropriateness, as well as sincerity — influential factors affecting employee motivation, company spirit, and productivity.

• Beware of confusing personal and professional

Manners will take you where money won't.

compliments in the workplace. Unless handled carefully, personal compliments at work can quickly turn into flattery, and flattery in today's workplace eventually works against good business practice. Giving flattery can put you at risk. Receiving it adds tension.

In business settings, a rule of thumb is compliment the action first, then the performer. Compliments up the chain of command on appearance — hair, clothes, figures — suggest currying favor, apple-polishing, and even less complimentary phrases. And frequent personal compliments from superior to subordinate breach the line of professional distance. Women question men who acknowledge their appearance and not their work.

• Work toward sincerity and spontaneity in giving compliments. Celebrate the good work of others quickly and directly.

People thrive on honest compliments. Manners will take you where money won't, and people work for more than money alone. Manners are good business practice.

Sometimes It Can Be Just As Good To Receive

Paul McClanahan, an architect formerly with Jackson, Miller, Brandt, Wilds & Associates, acknowledges the value of a good compliment and works to give and receive them well.

"It is and has been difficult for me to accept compliments. I tend to diminish my efforts. If someone compliments me, say, on a building's design, I do say 'Thank you,' but I add that it wasn't a big deal, when in fact I know it was a major effort. I am now conscious about saying 'Thank you' only."

McClanahan is not unlike other business professionals who struggle with accepting compliments.

While Ken Blanchard's *One Minute Manager* advocates one-minute commendation, it only touches on accepting praise. Etiquette guidelines coach individuals in the workplace to give and receive compliments well. This skill is a valuable business asset. It conveys confidence in oneself and one's work, and it expresses gratitude.

When you accept a compliment well, you honor the giver.

Here are some tips on receiving compliments well:

• Say "Thank you." Guard against mumbling about how old something is, what flaws it has, or that anyone else could have done it. When you accept a compliment well, you honor the giver. It hangs in the air for everyone to enjoy.

• Don't return a compliment with a compliment. It detracts from the goodwill of the person who initiated the comment. It also implies an obligation (on your part) to return the favor.

• Believe the good people see in you. Compliments bolster your self-esteem and filter criticism so that when criticism comes, as it certainly will, it isn't crippling.

•Record compliments. Documenting what you do well is a wise business practice, professionally and personally. This record reminds you during times of doubt that on this day, this person said you did this well.

Respected Professionals Fulfill Obligations Of Their Positions

Have you ever had committee members, appointed or volunteer, contribute in name only or occupy a valuable position but not participate?

Ever have leading members of your group or organization just happen to be busy during important planning meetings but ever present during public events?

Can you never reach the people you need to speak with, and do you give up on leaving messages?

The hallmarks of an effective and respected business professional are being available, accepting responsibility for commitments, participating in unglamorous tasks required to get things done, and being there during critical times to honor people and the work they do.

Now, that doesn't mean you call meetings too often or at inopportune times then wail that no one cares or comes. Or that as a participant, you must be present at every event.

The hallmarks of an effective and respected business professional are being available, accepting responsibility for commitments, participating in unglamorous tasks required to get things done, and being there during critical times to honor people and the work they do.

But it does mean that you develop the judgment to know which events are more important than others and when just your presence lends support.

Here is a checklist to determine your availability:

• Do you participate in most of the meetings and apologize for missing those you are unable to attend, or do you not respond to meeting notices or phone calls at all?

• Do you participate willingly in companywide events that are meant to build the team, or do you create excuses not to attend, not to blend?

• Are you overcommitted? Do you hold your appointment for the prestige only and not offer your resignation if you sense you are interfering more than contributing?

Take stock of your contributions. Be aware of positions held for pride and those held for results. Be willing to contribute or let go.

Reserving Judgment Creates Opportunity

Today's business philosophy in this fast-paced world supports being proactive, decisive, and risk-taking.

Yet, at times, business professionals may find the wiser course is to reserve judgment. I'm not talking about procrastination, indecisiveness, or cowardice. I'm talking about being open to impressions, to information from unusual sources, to innovation.

Many times we are forced to make, or even demand of ourselves, premature judgments in which we categorize ideas, people, and projects as "good or bad," "priority or back-burner," or in other "either-or" terms.

Yet premature judgment can be divisive and shortsighted. It can undermine productivity, creativity, trust, and respect. Part of the breadth of a consummate business professional is the ability to control judgment. Business professionals need to be aware of how preconceived judgments undermine the ability of groups to solve problems.

For example, a recent gathering of Leadership South Carolina, a statewide program for existing and emerging leaders to explore some of the toughest issues facing South Carolina, examined how prejudging set limitations to their problem-solving. During the orientation session, Dr. LaVeta Small, a faculty member of USC's Criminal Justice Department, and a

There are times when by withholding judgment you are exercising it.

team of group-process professionals led the class through what she describes as a "series of exercises specifically designed to create openness to diverse perspectives and backgrounds, and to surface initial resistance, even prejudice and stereotypes about people, places, and the work they do."

The group wrestles with labeling: urban/rural, Yankee/Southerner, black/white, public/private, and male/female. The purpose of the exercise is to address these preconceived notions which tend to polarize individuals, groups, and communities, and prevent resolution of important issues of the day.

This LSC exercise calls to mind how we limit ourselves and squander opportunities by jumping to conclusions and making judgments too early in our own lives and work. Here are some tips to guard against this:

• Look for opportunities in which you can listen without evaluating. Just absorb the information. Let things season.

• Take an inventory of how you might prejudge the value of people and ideas and when you might be guilty of limited expectations. Hold yourself accountable to a sense of fair play and open-mindedness.

There are times when by withholding judgment you are exercising it. Be known for having judgment. It is an unassailable business asset.

Maintaining Contact Solidifies Professional Relations

Lately, when I've asked groups of professionals to list the traits they admire in business people, "accessibility" is named.

Everyone is familiar with the phrase, "manage by wandering around" and its obvious benefits. But often, with so much to do — meetings to attend, problems to solve, projects to complete — we get out of the habit. Yet it continues to be appreciated by staff and customers and is time well spent.

"You can't cater to your clients and watch your staff fall apart. You get resentful if you can't get to the boss, or the only time you see each other is when there is a problem," says Rosanne G. Clementi, Senior Ecologist/Permitting Coordinator for Biological Research Associates in Tampa.

"Several of us work independently, but we have to guard against isolating ourselves. We need to physically spend time together, not a lot, just enough to feel a part of the group, so we don't feel abandoned. Supervisors need to pay attention to their employees, even when employees don't think they need

"Supervisors need to pay attention to their employees, even when employees don't think they need it."

it." Here's a checklist to evaluate your accessibility:

• Be deliberate about returning phone calls. Don't be the voice message phantom. Let people know when you'll be in and ask them to let you know when would be a good time to reach them.

• Schedule office hours so that people know generally when you will be in and open for questions, not rushing to your next meeting or hurrying them to make a point. Make your office physically welcoming and accessible, not hidden by heavy doors, long corridors, or several secretaries.

• Get out among the troops without a crisis to manage or a critical eye. Make your agenda to visit. Ask, "How's your job? What can we do to help you?" Wear less formal clothing so that you don't appear formidable.

Be aware of how difficult you are to reach. Sure, there are times to close the door, but guard against being so busy you forget how important it is for people to have access to you.

Reciprocity Is An Important Part Of Good Business Relationships

We Americans are casual about reciprocating professional courtesies, to a point.

We are generally quick to extend favors, issue invitations, and offer advice or leads to help each other. We don't expect repayment and are offended or hurt when someone feels obligated to balance the books for a gesture we offered as goodwill. We even consider it a privilege to be asked to return a favor to someone who has been especially generous to us.

But we are suspicious of people who expect reciprocity, who mention too early what you can do for them if they do this for you, who frequently refer to what people owe them, and who hint of future obligations.

And we are aware of those individuals and groups who ask for help but never offer, who consistently accept invitations but never initiate or serve as hosts, who return strong referrals with weak ones.

We see ourselves and our American ways quite clearly in contrast to the Japanese, who are extremely serious about social

We consider it a privilege to be asked to return a favor to someone who has been especially generous to us.

and business reciprocity.

Their rules are precise. Gestures, gifts, and invitations among individuals or corporations must be reciprocated in kind and as soon as possible. Favors are asked with the expectation of equal repayment, and the score is precisely kept.

Betty Pleasant, senior sales manager with Disney Group Events in Orlando, Fla., described her awareness of reciprocity, or lack of it, in her work.

"I see companies offer special packages to individuals in hopes of getting the business they represent, but the individuals accept it for personal use with no realistic intention of working with them," she said. "I see weak leads offered for strong ones, and the word gets around about these individuals, just as it does for those who pass along information you can count on."

Be aware of reciprocity in business relationships. Know when you need to repay, when you need to initiate, and when you need to refuse.

Show Sensitivity During Times Of Bereavement

"Business must be run from the mind," a friend recently told me. "Objective, analytical. If it is run from the heart or stomach, decisions are not always reliable."

Yet, there are times in our business lives which call for us to respond from the heart, especially when we must respond to a death. Here is a review of how to respond appropriately and sincerely to the death of a business associate or those deeply affected by the tragedy:

• Consider the needs of the bereaved. Whether you write, pay a condolence call, or direct the activities of the mourning, keep in the top of your mind what would be most comforting to those grieving. Seek a low profile. Resist calling attention to yourself. Quietly perform kind gestures or offer help.

• Attend the funeral if it is open. Your presence may not be remembered individually, but collectively is a source of com-

There are times in our business lives which call for us to respond from the heart.

fort to those experiencing the loss. Plus, you can advance your own grief process.

Companies that enable their employees to attend funerals of coworkers and their families are admired for their compassion and sensitivity.

• Follow up in the weeks and months after the death. Be attentive during holidays. You can acknowledge birthdays, even the anniversary of the death, by sending a special note. It doesn't have to directly refer to the death, but might read simply: "Thinking of You." Don't be overly solicitous, cast concerned looks their way, or intrude by repeatedly asking the bereaved how they are and if everything is all right.

Responding sincerely and appropriately to a death is an expected behavior. Through your actions, you indicate your sensitivity, your depth of character, and your integrity.

Businesses Need To Be Mindful Of Bias Regardless Of Intention

The other day, I was looking through a promotional piece for a local business and saw all white faces, with a female staff standing around men in high back chairs (as if in attendance).

That same week, I was also told about:

- "Sexretaries."
- About men who routinely call women with whom they work "babe," "honey," "dear," and "sweetie," and find all kinds of ways to slip their arms around women's waists.
- About clients who, when assigned to female professionals, "want to see the person really in charge."
- About not wanting to include women in certain activities of a public organization because it is the "last place men gather alone."

Polished business professionals — and the companies they represent — need to be mindful of bias that may exist, whether intended or not. To prevent being prejudiced, or perceived as

Include people of both sexes to represent your organization and make strategic decisions.

such, you can:

• Diplomatically, but directly correct inappropriate spoken or written language.

• Include people of both sexes to represent your organization and make strategic decisions. Avoid the prejudicial statement, "I just couldn't find anyone qualified," or "I respect women, I really do, but. . .."

• Ask your employees and customers to let you know when you might be considered biased. Believe me. They will tell you.

As the workplace becomes more and more diverse, and the labor shortage presses in, a limited view on the roles of women, or anyone for that matter, will cripple your ability to recruit and retain qualified workers, even attract customers.

People watch. They know when bias exists. Work to have your policies, your outlook, above reproach.

Businesses Reveal True Character By Showing Social Responsibility

Disasters such as Hurricane Hugo always reveal the depth of character of individuals who make quick decisions about what they can do to help and then take action.

They also reveal the character of businesses who recognize and act on their social responsibility. Commitment to the common good is what the public admires in a company and what bonds employees to the workplace.

Like many others, one company in Columbia quietly responded to the public good in the manner in which they were able—sending food and water to several disaster sites, contributing a substantial sum of money to the effort, matching cash contributions of their employees, and donating employees to aid in the relief effort.

A simple in-house memo detailed the action the company had taken. Employees not only felt a sense of pride about their own individual efforts, but also pride in their company.

Whether responding to a crisis or addressing the ongoing social issues in a community, large and small companies can

Commitment to the common good is what the public admires in a company and what bonds employees to the workplace.

actively search for opportunities to be a good public citizen.

Etiquette strategies for the public good include:

• Responding rapidly to crisis. This is when leadership reveals its depth — when knowing what to do is matched with quick action.

• Contributing cash donations and matching those by the employees.

• Donating company products, services, and facilities, such as computers, printing, meeting rooms, and accounting ability. Take an inventory of what you have and what you do and offer it. Donate employees' time and encourage routine voluntarism.

• Establishing a system to sustain community support. Keep philanthropy prevalent not just in the mission statement of the business, but also in the objectives of individual departments and employees.

The dividends of supporting the common good are exponential. Make sure you do your part.

Business World May Be Big, But There's No Room For Chauvinism

Tammis Hunter, a graduate student at the University of Texas at Austin, describes her former boss with disdain.

"He'd yell down the hall, 'Tammy, get your — in here,' and brag about what a chauvinist he was. He constantly discussed how women looked and had an incredible repertoire of sex jokes. He should have been an embarrassment to the company, but he's still there. I'm not."

It's unfortunate, but some people just don't know how to behave around professional women.

Jeff Roberts, who plans seminars for the Greensboro Institute of Internal Auditors in North Carolina, expresses a growing sentiment: "I was brought up to treat a lady like a lady, but things have changed. I don't want to make obvious mistakes that offend women."

With the changing roles of women, it is sometimes hard to know what is business etiquette and what is social etiquette, but those individuals who know the difference have an advantage. To avoid confusing or offending others, here are a few tips concerning etiquette between men and women in the workplace:

• In a business situation when only one woman is present, there is no need to defer to her, or for her to expect deference,

With the changing roles of women, it is sometimes hard to know what is business etiquette and what is social etiquette, but those individuals who know the difference have an advantage.

because she is the only woman present. In business, position and authority override gender. Also, the group should not expect her to speak for all women. If the group wants to know what women think, it might invite more women to the meeting.

• Women complain that many men offer them weak handshakes, or worse, presume familiarity with hugs and kisses — "Hey, baby. Don't give me a handshake. I deserve a hug!" Firm, quickly offered handshakes are the appropriate business greeting between men and women. Save hugs for the cocktail party.

• Although men were taught not to use profanity in mixed company, men who do use it, then apologize to women with a simpering, "Oh, I forgot there were ladies present," really offend. Either use it or don't, but don't single out women for the apologies.

• People who use "honey," "sweetie," "young ladies," and "girls" when referring to adult women should realize how ridiculous they sound. And avoid saying, "She just isn't tough enough," to eliminate women from jobs. That phrase has come to be considered blatantly sexist.

Hunter concludes, "We're not just genders here. We're people. The issue is treating people, regardless of their gender, with consideration and regard."

Small Talk Could Result In Big Business

The term "small talk" usually calls to mind superficial, meaningless conversation which wastes time until more important events arise.

Yet, astute business professionals recognize the value of these short conversations for creating goodwill and establishing a basis for further associations.

Simply put, people like to be around people who are easy to talk with. Translated into business terms, people will buy from, open accounts with, and approve projects for people who have mastered their field and refined the art of visiting.

But the common act of conversation can be a struggle for even the most accomplished business professional. So, how should we talk to people?

One of my most admired conversationalists is John Bernardin, a sales representative for 31 years with Thompson Dental Company. He has mastered the art of easy conversation. The skills he has developed are grounded in what he calls "common sense" but which are also common courtesies worth repeating.

Astute business professionals recognize the value of these short conversations for creating goodwill and establishing a basis for further associations.

• Adapt each conversation to the person to whom you are speaking. Keep conversations fresh and respond to the dynamics of the situation, otherwise you will soon be repeating yourself and boring others.

• Be casual and personal. Keep subjects light initially. Give people room to get to know you.

• Find the interests and needs of others. Just listen. Then ask questions about what people tell you.

• Work to find something nice to say about someone. "But it must be genuine," says Bernardin. "Halfhearted truths can reverse any progress you make."

• Try not to criticize anyone. In terms of gossip, Bernardin is guided by an old saying, "Great minds discuss ideas. Average minds discuss things, and low minds discuss people."

• Be yourself, but be your best self. No need to intentionally tell people the negatives about yourself. They might believe it. Self-deprecating humor is done well only by a skillful few.

Office Chitchat Doesn't Have To Be Idle Talk

Business relationships are formed by various means, but their success hinges on how people get along.

A major factor in developing a relationship is how people talk to one another, be it client, coworker, or boss. People treat business conversation too casually, which may cause unnecessary problems.

Etiquette can provide guidelines for everyday conversation in the workplace. These guidelines can increase your leverage or build confidence and enable you to respond to questions that need to be recognized as rude.

Mike Blackwell, president of Syncom, a communications venture and voice-processing company, makes it his business to analyze business conversations. His studies prove that 25 percent to 40 percent of business conversation is not business-related, and within those numbers fall meaningful and non-meaningful conversation.

"We encourage chitchat in the office if it builds relationships," Blackwell said. "It builds relationships if it leads to our getting to know more about a person's job function or reveals a person's values or feelings. This is helpful in our business."

Use the following as a guideline for basic business conversations:

Distinguish between friendliness and friendship in the workplace. Strive to be friendly, but don't misinterpret this as becoming friends.

• Distinguish between friendliness and friendship in the workplace. People at work should strive to be friendly, but don't misinterpret this as becoming friends. A polite distance can give you control and objectivity.

• Keep conversation businesslike. Most work environments are close quarters, and people are quickly affected by situations which become too personal. During business hours, keep a tight rein on conversation relating to personal matters.

• Subjects inappropriate for business conversation are asking why people haven't married or had children, or recounting your personal life or problems. Dead-end or silly topics include people's ages, dieting, health, the cost of living, and gossip.

• If someone asks you an offensive question, lightly brush it off. People sometimes don't know they are treading on sensitive subjects. Let them save face.

However, if they continue to probe, use a nice pause with direct eye contact to let them know they are out of bounds. Say, "I'd rather not talk about it now. Let's talk later." Then change the subject. If they persist, you can raise the stakes by telling them they are out of line.

"It's all in sensing what is appropriate," Blackwell said. "That's using good business judgment."

Small Talk Is A Business Skill That Makes Sense

October is conference season, when business professionals reach deep into their bag of business social skills before departing to spend three days with several hundred people at a regional convention. Individuals with strong social skills take advantage of new opportunities and come away with business contacts, cooperative work agreements, closed sales, even friendships. Those without, curse the process, huddle in their rooms, and eat alone.

Developing conversation aptitude (or the art of small talk) is one of those social skills that makes sense in business. As one friend confided under the promise of anonymity, "I went recently to a regional conference where I was the only one from my agency to attend. At lunch, I was all right, but in the evening, especially during the receptions, I really struggled to find someone to talk to. It's hard enough for me to walk up to a group of strangers, much less talk with them when I don't know them."

The second chapter of Letitia Baldridge's newest book, *Complete Guide to a Great Social Life* is one of the best I have read on how to start and maintain a conversation. Her pointers will build the confidence of even the most accomplished business executive.

Here are some of her suggestions, as well as a few of mine:

"It's hard enough for me to walk up to a group of strangers, much less talk with them when I don't know them."

• Take inventory of your strengths. Preoccupation with your inabilities forecasts failure. Visualize yourself as an interesting person. Then you can concentrate on others.

• Prepare several newsworthy, non-threatening topics you could talk about. Keep the tone positive. Find something complimentary to say about a person's profession, their company, or an associate.

• Approach individuals or couples, rather than groups. Why not move toward the most attractive or interesting person in the room? Treat yourself. Have some fun. Second choice, pick out someone who might be like you, someone of the same age, someone who might even be experiencing the same things you are.

• Concentrate while you listen to people. Focus on what they are saying. Respond to their words or the tone in which they express themselves.

• In a strained conversation, it's fine to decide that you might not enjoy talking with this person. The problem may not be with you, but with your partner. You don't have to always please. Just move on.

Conversational skills are a valuable business asset and confidence builder. They are learnable, but they do take preparation and practice.

Profanity Reflects Poorly On The Individual And The Company

I have resisted this column for months. But the issue surfaces regularly, almost predictably, in the seminars I present.

When I ask a group of business professionals what behaviors they consider rude, what behaviors are distracting, unproductive, and offensive, someone will say, almost grim-faced, "Profanity."

One of the fundamental rules in etiquette is to be deliberate about how you express yourself, to speak clearly and select words that will convey your message in a manner to be understood by your audience.

Undoubtedly some of you will snicker, "That is exactly what profanity does." But I am not talking about a few "hells" and "damns" or other words that burst in anger and then fade. I am talking about profanity that insults, that berates, that occurs in every sentence in every conversation, that is a weak attempt to add emphasis, and a poor excuse for word choice.

John Soldati, manager of corporate trust for Citizens & Southern Trust Co., tells two stories that helped shape his approach to profanity. Some 20 years ago in the Charlotte YMCA, he was cursing loudly about his poor handball play.

" I am convinced profanity is uncalled for in the business place. Solid managers don't need it."

The venerable director, the late Harry Welch, heard him and came to stand by his court, John thought to watch his play. "But after the game, Mr. Welch took me aside to say essentially, 'John, you are the kind of person we want in the Y, but that kind of behavior and language demeans you.' He meant the work I did and the corporation I represented at the time.

"Then, several years later, as I was giving a presentation, I added unnecessary profanity to the prepared text, and afterwards, one of the participants came up to me to tell me she thought the content was strong, '... but the language you chose wasn't applicable to the subject, and furthermore, it doesn't become you.'

"It has made me conscious of the use of profanity ever since. I don't see the merit in it, and I hate using it. People use it for emphasis when it really detracts, and the costs in loss of respect and poor reflection on the corporation and the individual are too high. I am convinced it is uncalled for in the business place. Solid managers don't need it."

Be aware of the purpose of your profanity — what you stand to gain, but also what you risk.

Saying "No" Tactfully Can Soothe Sensitive Situations

We all admire people who in sensitive situations know what to do or say to protect the self-esteem of others.

In business, tact is an especially esteemed skill when we discipline ourselves to be fast, direct, decisive, and oriented to the bottom line.

The frustration comes in knowing when and how to use it. What situations require tact? Not all do. And what are the steps to being tactful and avoiding the reputation of a "confrontation dodger"?

One situation where tact surely can be a business asset is in telling people "no." While refusing requests, funding, invitations, or employment is essential to business, in an economy more focused on ethics and service, how you refuse can determine your success in precious future relationships.

Here are a few "how-tos" for telling people "no."

• Consider the best method of delivery. Does the refusal require the formality of a letter, or would a quiet conversation

The person you refuse today may be in the position to refuse you tomorrow.

to the side avoid embarrassment and allow the request to quickly fade?

• Agree when you can and thank people for asking. Say, "Your credentials are admirable," or "Thank you for inviting me to be a part of your program." This shows that you acknowledge and honor the request.

• Explain the reason for refusal before the actual refusal is expressed. And make your reasons specific, sincere, and short, but not blunt. Generalities invite suspicion and often lead to being long-winded.

• Tell people what you can do for them and what they can do to have their request fulfilled. Suggest alternatives: "Try us again in six months." "We can't grant the 6,000 you requested, but we can handle 4,000." Project a spirit of cooperation and avoid appearing smug.

Turning people down is not always an easy task. But it becomes easier if you consider that the person you refuse today may be in the position to refuse you tomorrow.

Year End Listening Requires Special Care

The art of listening, while valuable year round, can be especially important during end-of-year reports. These evaluations focus upon product value, workforce productivity, and service effectiveness.

However, not all work conversation is report giving, project updates, and percentage of quota summaries. At the year's end, we focus on our accomplishments, our progress, and our effectiveness. We tend to become introspective and evaluate the meaning of our work. Conversations with coworkers, friends, and family often become personal. These conversations may require more listening rather than talking.

A good listener stands apart from his or her peers and is respected for that special ability. Poor listening, on the other hand, can limit your effectiveness as a business professional and your sensitivity as a human being. Here are some tips that may help you:

Unless asked to offer it, withhold advice. People have to find their own solutions.

• Listen without evaluating. Pay attention to ideas, to emotions behind the words. If you push for the facts or deny the issue, you suppress the conversation. Although you may only be trying to help, you may appear argumentative and judgmental instead. Get people to continue to talk by responding to their feelings.

• Unless asked to offer it, withhold advice. More often than not, people just want sounding boards. They have to find their own solutions. Yours won't always work for them.

• Work to understand. Be with people, not do for them. Be patient. Wait people out. When you say, "The same thing happened to me. . . ," you are talking about yourself when people want to talk about their lives.

Listening is a skill that will serve you well. It will distinguish you. It seems that part of maturing is talking less and listening more.

In Business, Your Best Moves Are Often Their Moves

One of the most basic, yet elegant ways etiquette is applied is in establishing rapport. The faster you establish rapport and build credibility in the business world, the faster you "close the sale" or convince someone. But how do you do this without appearing obvious, overbearing, or too eager to please?

• Match people's speech and their pace. Pay attention to what people say and how they say it. Work their favorite words into your conversation. If they are animated, add more expression and gestures. If they take time with their thoughts and words, slow down your responses. This forces you to be more in tune with others.

• Wait for people to finish their thoughts. This will catapult you to success with people. But if you don't do this, you will crash in failure. Make a pact: "No interruptions, no volunteering."

• Mirror people's body language. If they put their forearms

Pay attention to what people say and how they say it.

on the table, gradually move yours there. If they shift their weight, move with them. Try it the next time you submit your budget for approval. It works!

Although these actions may strike you as arbitrary, they have been proven statistically to increase your odds of doing business well. Alan Washington, a Columbia-based psychotherapist, verifies these skills as components of an innovative psychological strategy call "neurolinguistic programming."

Washington uses neurolinguistic programming, or NLP, to put his clients at ease and increase the effectiveness of therapy.

From the moment you meet people, through ongoing encounters, be deliberate in developing rapport. Washington urges, "Make it conscious, something you chose to do." As you practice, you'll nurture important ingredients for a good working relationship: rapport, credibility, confidence, and respect.

Telephone Rudeness Rings In People's Minds

One of the top three topics I am requested to address in my seminars is telephone manners. Believe it! Everyone has a favorite rude telephone story.

I suppose people are careless with telephone style because they are busy, in a hurry, or because being unable to see anyone helps them believe no one notices them. But they do.

Breaches of telephone etiquette transcend organizational hierarchy and range from smacking gum, to not returning calls, to refusing to take messages.

Consider the results of a UCLA communications survey three years ago. The survey found that in spoken messages we convey seven percent of the message from the words we choose, 38 percent from the way we say them, and 55 percent from body language. Now remove the influence of body language (which is what you do when you talk on the telephone), and you can see how important your word choice and speaking manner are.

Seibels Bruce Insurance Co. recently focused its training

> **"The telephone is the first intro-
> duction customers have to our
> company. We must be positive,
> courteous, and produce a good
> first impression."**

efforts on improving telephone style companywide. Training Director Ann Muir says, "The telephone is the first introduction customers have to our company. We must be positive, courteous, and produce a good first impression."

General tips include:

• Work to make your voice clear. Put endings on your words. To distinguish each word and prevent garbling, visualize commas between your words: "Why, don't, we, meet?"

• Return phone calls within 24 hours, even to those with whom you don't want to talk, or get one of your staff to return the call. Otherwise, people think you didn't get their message, and you perpetuate the chase.

•Say "Good-bye," not "Bye," or "Bye-bye." "Good-bye" is crisp in business; the others sound fluffy.

Pay attention to how you use the telephone. It makes a difference. Your choice to handle it well can either advance or obstruct your carefully-crafted business image.

Rudeness On The Telephone Is A Major Hang-Up Of Businesses

It's time for another telephone etiquette column because in asking working professionals what business etiquette issues concern them most, they always list telephone rudeness first or second.

"It is my firm belief that someone has sent out a memo indicating that it is acceptable behavior to put people on hold and never pick up the phone again," writes J. Smith Harrison, vice president of market development of Seibels Bruce Insurance Co.

"I have noted in several organizations that receptionists are quick to ask who you are, who you are with, and what you want. Then they put you on hold — never to return," Harrison writes.

The following are telephone tips that will prevent you from sending people into orbit:

• Don't keep people on hold for more than 30 seconds and asking who is calling in an arrogant, curt tone.

Harrison describes a recent experience that went like this: "(Hold). . .Whom may I say is calling? (Hold). . .In reference to? (Hold). . .Oh, he isn't in." End of conversation.

• Ask people's permission to be put on hold. Project a helpful manner. Offer the caller a good time of day to reach the

*Return telephone calls within 24 hours.
Beyond that time, people think you
either didn't get the message or that
you don't care.*

person. Suggest to callers that their calls are important to the receiver. Say, "I'm sorry. She's not in. Is there anything I can help you with?" If the receiver is working on a special project or will be out of town, explain that to the caller.

• Make sure your telephone system is updated to handle the calls you receive. Your receptionists can then do their jobs efficiently and be polite to callers.

• When you make a call, state your name and your business in a manner that can be understood and that is respectful of the person who answers. Don't be gimmicky, try to trick the receptionist, or snap, "No, you cannot tell her who is calling."

• Not returning phone calls. Do return telephone calls within 24 hours. Beyond that time, people think you either didn't get the message or that you don't care. Not calling back is plain rude.

If you are unable to return calls or don't want to talk to people, get someone in the office to do it for you. Tell them you don't have the information, or you are not interested, or try in again in six months.

Professionals in authority need to call their offices periodically to see how their phones are handled. Poor telephone etiquette is bad business.

Insistence Added To Persistence Are Often Met With Resistance

Three of the hallmarks of etiquette in business are treating people with dignity and respect, being aware of when they might be embarrassed, and not calling attention to the bad manners of others.

Sure we all know that, but here is how it can be demonstrated in everyday business life.

A client, supplier, or colleague you have tried to reach has not returned your phone call.

You leave messages and say you will call back. You continue to miss your party even at times suggested by their staff.

As a last resort, you leave your number and have mechanisms in place—receptionists, answering machines, voice mail —to receive the call if you aren't there. Still no reply, and it has been three weeks.

Finally, you reach the person. You preface your remarks

Be aware of pressing too hard when insisting on the courtesy of a reply.

with how you regret you haven't been able to reach each other, and they explode, saying they have most certainly been easy to reach and accuse you of harassing their staff.

You admit subtly that you wanted them to know how hard they were to reach, but the tables have turned and now you have somehow become the offender.

Betsy Hixson, a seasoned sales representative with Fisher Scientific in Atlanta, knows how to avoid these situations.

"I drop them a quick note. I'll leave them a message that unless I hear from them, I'll see them Thursday," she said.

"When I see them, I remain pleasant. I don't want them defensive. I assume they were busy, and I realize I am the one selling."

Be aware of pressing too hard when insisting on the courtesy of a reply.

Smooth Business Meetings Enhance Professional Credibility

You have seen it happen over and over. Reputations of business associates rise and fall, and few forums offer such an obvious view of the process as meetings do. How you handle yourself at meetings helps you increase the respect of your associates and enhances your effectiveness. Polished professionals see the value of meeting etiquette to keep the business process running smoothly and their personal credibility high.

Here is a basic review of meeting etiquette when you present a new idea:

• Consider the tone of the meeting. Is this the proper forum? Knowing when to present and when not to present new information indicates your good business judgment.

• Build support before the meeting. With the exception of an informal setting, present your ideas ahead of time to several individuals who will give you good feedback. Search for opposition by presenting it to someone with whom you usually

"Involving people in the process is a good idea because it makes you look like a problem solver, not a know-it-all."

disagree but who can give you reasons for failure you may not have thought about.

• Phrase your ideas clearly. Rehearse. Too often, business associates begin to speak, then falter, and really don't have a good idea in mind, only vague thoughts. Doing this too often erodes your credibility.

• Instead of phrasing suggestions in terms of "I think . . .," or "I have an idea . . .," state information with "What if we . . .," or "Would it make sense if . . .," to keep your ego in check and involve others in the process.

Cynthia Legette, a business writer and public relations consultant, says, "Involving people in the process is a good idea because it makes you look like a problem solver, not a know-it-all. Being known in meetings as a thinker, a good listener, and someone not afraid to voice opinions for fear of being wrong are good characteristics to develop."

Perfecting The Art Of Introducing Guest Speakers Is Worth The Effort

Recently, I've noticed several people do an exceptional job of introducing a speaker.

I admired how they presented their guest in flattering, but worthy and relevant terms, how they prepared the audience for a good experience, and how they set the stage for a successful outcome.

Jane Rutledge, a regional director of the National Spa & Pool Institute, is one who excels at introducing guest speakers. If you follow her example when you are asked to introduce a speaker at a luncheon, convention, or shareholder's meeting, you'll perform your task with as much style as she did:

• Make arrangements for a smooth arrival. Give good directions. Be on the lookout and welcome guest speakers warmly.

• Review audiovisual equipment, seating arrangements, and the schedule, especially when speakers should end. Ask what else they might need.

After these housekeeping duties, introduce them to important guests and brief them more thoroughly on your group and what you'd like to see happen.

• As you compose your remarks, remember your purpose

Resist the temptation to grandstand or treat the introduction too casually.

is to set the stage for a successful presentation. Praise or tease the audience. Get them ready. Focus on why the topic is important and why the speaker is qualified.

You might share a story about the time something happened to you or the speaker that relates to the topic. Resist the temptation to grandstand or treat the introduction too casually. And correctly pronounce names. Rehearse aloud if you must.

• Keep your program on schedule. Take action necessary to start and end on time. Give other speakers the hook. Get the food moving faster.

It is poor form to have speakers prepare a 40 minute presentation only for you to mismanage the schedule, forcing them to condense their remarks to 15 minutes. It is also disrespectful of the audience.

• Pay attention to how the program ends. Field questions and have a few yourself to lighten the tone if the discussion gets too heavy or if it gets off track. Thank the speaker, tell what you learned, and lead the applause.

You can distinguish yourself and achieve your mission with attention to small tasks. It's easy to do exceptional work. Why be ordinary?

Following Unstated Rules Will Increase Sales

In business, there is an etiquette to sales. And how well you follow the unstated rules influences your success or lack of it.

So much of the process is basic common courtesy, yet it is the basics that people become casual with and overlook. To review the dos and don'ts of selling, here is a quick checklist:

• Before the presentation, do prepare ahead of time. Call for an appointment. Organize your presentation around your client's needs.

• Be prepared to answer how your services and products will benefit them. Don't "kingpin" or organize your remarks around only how wonderful your product or service is.

• Assemble ahead of time what you will need for the presentation. Don't ask to borrow a copier, pencil, or paper. Have the appropriate brochures ready.

• Develop a professional business appearance. Dress to make your customer comfortable, but don't patronize them with underdressing or intimidate them with overdressing. Grooming should be impeccable.

**So much of the process is basic
common courtesy, yet it is the
basics that people become casual
with and overlook.**

• During the presentation, arrive on time, and if you are late, apologize.

• Treat receptionists with respect. Don't expect them to baby-sit or entertain you.

• When with your appointment, express appreciation for their time to see you, but don't apologize for taking up too much of their time.

• Act with dignity and pride for your work. Be friendly, but don't expect or try to be friends.

• Wait to be shown where to sit. Keep your briefcase on the floor or in your lap, not on their desk. Listen to the customers' needs. Don't talk just about what you have to offer.

• Respect their privacy. Offer to leave the room if they must take an important phone call, but if they wave for you to stay, be busy and indicate you are not eavesdropping. And don't refer to the phone conversation after it has finished.

• Learn to deal with rejection gracefully. It is part of the job. Place yourself to be considered favorably next time.

Buyers Can Help Set The Tone For Fair Dealing And Good Service

Just as there is an etiquette for selling, there is an etiquette for buying.

To recount appropriate behavior for the purchaser or the client, here are a few etiquette tips to preserve your service:

• Let your vendors know the depth of your interest. Some customers will exercise polite avoidance, rather than tell a supplier "no." Others will use free evaluative services and then decide not to buy.

Both strategies, if practiced consistently, even in the name of tough negotiating, are insincere and deceptive. Over time, they can undermine your reputation among suppliers and affect your service.

• Honor appointments you make. Look as if you are expecting your guest. Don't sigh and shove your papers to the side with a let's-get-this-over-with attitude.

• Apologize for keeping sales representatives waiting. You may have limited time to meet with them, and you need not

Let your vendors know the depth of your interest.

exceed that, but be respectful, pay attention, and act interested for the time you have promised.

• Hold calls and interruptions. If you must rush, offer to reschedule.

• Accept a fair price. Some suppliers have earned the right to charge the prices they do. Persistently needling prices to wear down your supplier may backfire.

• Pay on time. Customers play the strangest games with suppliers and vendors. They and their systems stall payment sometimes because they don't have the funds. While this is often true, other times it is because they want the feeling of being in power as the buyer.

Whether the supplier is a large company or cottage industry, individuals within the company can be personally penalized by late payments.

Evaluate how you treat your suppliers and vendors. Do your part to set the tone for fair dealing and good service.

In Business, Put Your Best Look Forward

One of the easiest, most effective, most character revealing practices business professionals can adopt is to be attentive, really attentive, to business appearance— dressing, grooming, and general carriage.

When I began this business, I touched only lightly on the subject in the seminars I presented. Now, however, I devote considerable time to the discussion of an individual's physical business image.

First, this topic is one of the top two I am requested to address. Secondly, mastery, which is so simple, controls how people react to you and helps you project your best self.

Mary Hewlette, a partner in the Hilton Head law firm of Hewlette and Hewlette, expressed the value of a good business appearance:

"Being well-groomed can tell so much about you. It conveys that you are organized and disciplined, that you care about others and not about offending them, that you care about yourself and have a good self-image. And it doesn't cost anything. Everyone from all walks of life can do something about it."

Here is a review of the basics for even the most polished

"Being well-groomed can tell so much about you. It conveys that you are organized and disciplined, that you care about others and not about offending them, that you care about yourself and have a good self-image. And it doesn't cost anything."

professional:

• Keep your nails in good condition. People watch your hands. Be sure nails are clean and a reasonable length—no bitten stumps, no ragged edges. For women, polish should not be a distracting color or chipped.

• Keep your hair well-trimmed, clean, and away from your face. Update your style if you haven't for a while. It projects a progressive image and creates an impression of consistency.

• Avoid any heavy fragrance in the workplace. Ask a good friend if you wear too much. Heavy colognes and perfumes evoke more complaints than any other grooming issue. Wash your hands after you apply fragrance. And be attentive to deodorant. No fragrance can disguise a lack of basic hygiene.

• Keep your clothes mended, clean, and well-pressed. Look them over carefully. Are buttons missing? Are there spots you think no one notices? Do your clothes fit? Do they look overly worn? Everyone respects neatness in collars, shirts, and cuffs.

Your success in the business world is affected by how people perceive you. And good grooming, which affects that perception, is one thing you can control to your advantage.

When Employees Look Sloppy, Don't Dress Up Your Warning.

When supervisors discuss how to counsel staff on grooming and dress, they give a wide range of approaches.

The first method is to ignore it, and maybe it will go away.

There's the hot potato method: "You tell her." "No, you tell her."

Then there's the no warning method: "Your dress is inappropriate for our work here, and unless you change, we'll find a replacement."

Although many of us understand the importance of dress and grooming, some people still haven't learned it.

It isn't vanity, it's making a good visual impression.

Dr. Albert Mehrabian of UCLA's psychology department found that 55 percent of our message is conveyed by how we look when we speak.

Dress standards are not limited to people in certain professions. Dressing well is just as important for the back room clerks as it is for the customer service representative on the front line.

Dressing well is just as important for the back room clerks as it is for the customer service representative on the front lines.

A company's dress policy applies to individuals who dress to distract or bend the rules and to employees who wear uniforms.

Chuck Carreon, manager of branch operations of BankAmerica in Los Angeles, says his company has a dress code. "It's reasonable, specific, and supported by the company," he said. "We tell people about it during the interview process.

"If people dress inappropriately, we send them home and tell them to change and return in 30 minutes. We even schedule a casual day periodically to boost employee morale."

As a manager, you need to take responsibility to counsel employees about their dress. You should develop a strong policy that takes you off the spot. Your policy can be casual, but nobody wants sloppy. If you have to call an employee on inappropriate dress, be specific. Tell them what's wrong with their attire.

Don't apologize for enforcing your policy. Be consistent.

Good Leisure Skills Reflect Good Business Skills

Situations in business call you to display skills for which you may not have been formally trained, but skills which are increasingly becoming expected business behaviors.

As the ties between the business community and the arts grow stronger, cultural events are becoming forums for business and pleasure. David Bass, audit manager with Arthur Andersen & Co., acknowledges that as professionals rise in an organization and become part of an executive team, "Expectations of you by your firm and your clients change. Relationships are maintained at a different level.

At times, it's so clear that people at the top of the business world prefer to work with professionals who are well-rounded. We can't always, and don't want always, to talk about the latest technical accounting pronouncements."

As we participate in the arts, we find we enjoy it and increase our visibility and goodwill. And we see more and more clients at the events.

Some techniques to help you handle and enjoy these events are:

• Arrive in time to check your coats, get preliminary visiting

People at the top of the business world prefer to work with professionals who are well-rounded.

out of the way, decide who will sit where, read your program, and get settled in your seats. Good ushers will help you be seated at appropriate times and prevent you from disturbing others. Respect their lead. Don't argue. And watch for the signal to return to your seat after intermission.

• Be quiet. We all hear whispering, crackly paper, beepers, jingly jewelry, snappy purses, and alarm watches. That's not the kind of attention you want drawn to yourself.

• Clap at appropriate times. Spontaneous applause can be a genuine display of your appreciation, but it can disturb the performers. Applaud (generally) after a complete dance, aria, selection, or scene. Acknowledge individual artists at the end of the entire performance, not as they enter and exit the stage during the performance. You do applaud as conductors and featured concert artists take their places. If you are unsure, take your cue from the rest of the audience.

Above all, support the arts. Not only do they serve as forums for business, but participating broadens your perspective. And it's fun!

Table Manners Are An Important Business Skill

Today's business professionals and the companies they represent invest more than $210 billion annually in training and development to build the technical and human relations skills required to do a job well.

But one area where the investment is thin, yet where business is increasingly done, is at the table. And table manners is an area where people often have problems.

Elizabeth Jones, manager and consultant with Discovery Toys in Columbia, recounts a typical story. She just returned from her company's annual meeting, attended by more than 900 participants.

During the luncheon meetings she said, "Everything was so confusing. When do you start eating with a table of 15? Things were being passed all different ways. I thought I knew what to do, but other people had different ideas."

Command of the dining process, be it at a small business lunch with clients or a convention meeting with several hundred participants, is just one of those business skills you have

Mastery of basic table manners will boost not only your company's business image, but also your confidence and success.

to know.

Basic guidelines include:

• Put your napkin in your lap as soon as you are seated, unless you are the guest, then you follow the host's lead.

• Pass to the right. If you start the rolls around the table, offer one to the person on your left, then start it to the right.

• At a table with more than eight people and no designated host, begin eating when three or four people around you are served. Of course, if you haven't been served, you would be polite by urging those who have been served to "Please, go ahead."

• Pace your eating. Take medium-sized bites and chew with your mouth closed. People do notice the gobblers, gulpers, and smackers of the world, and their behaviors are discussed.

Mastery of basic table manners will boost not only your company's business image, but also your confidence and success.

Being In Charge From The Start Avoids Awkwardness At Tab Time

When I spoke to college athletes recently, a football player asked what he should do about women who invite him to dinner and say they will pay.

He said he didn't know what to do. He felt awkward because it was against his upbringing. Then, from across the room, another player shouted, "Let her pay! Let her pay!"

The same idea can apply to business where women are required to entertain clients, sponsor business events, and take customers to lunch.

The process can be clumsy for men and women. Men may be reluctant to let a woman pay or may feel uncomfortable as the guest. Women may send mixed signals about their role as host or may not pick up the check when it is their turn.

Here are typical behaviors that work for hosts for a business lunch:

• Initiate the invitation. Let the other party know the general purpose of your get-together. Say you would like them

Knowing the roles of a host and a guest can make business run smoother. It removes the little glitches that interfere with the business at hand.

to be your guest.

• Hosts take the lead by suggesting one or two locations they know will appeal to most guests, where they know the quality of the food and can suggest specials, and where the restaurant knows them and can help them act as hosts. Wavering on location sends mixed messages about who is in charge.

• Approve the table offered to you and indicate where your guest is to sit. You will want to be in the position to signal the server, but offer the preferred banquette seats to your guests.

• Suggest items they might enjoy. Address the server and give him or her the table instructions.

• To reduce questions about payment, arrange the billing ahead of time. The server can bring you the ticket with the gratuity already added. You can quickly check it over for accuracy and sign the check. Guests can offer to pay, but not insist, nor do they need to get the tip.

Proper Tipping Adds To Your Credibility

"Why don't we get together for lunch Thursday to see what we can do to bring this deal to a close?"

You meet at a familiar restaurant. You spread your papers across the table. Your briefcases occupy extra chairs. You quickly order meals and get right to business. Your food arrives in a timely manner. You eat. The plates are removed. Two hours later, you close the deal, and the check comes. Now what?

Many restaurateurs and the servers they employ often tell me their patrons pay the bill, get up and leave, and either undertip or don't tip at all.

Tipping says a lot about who you are. By knowing the customs and, yes, etiquette of tipping, you add credibility to your business persona. Knowing how to handle the ending, as well as the beginning and middle of a business meal, indicates your attention to detail and your investment in your professional life.

People who knowingly undertip are more miserly than

Knowing how to handle the ending as well as the beginning and middle of a business meal indicates your attention to detail and your investment in your professional life.

frugal. And the word gets around. Why risk cultivating that kind of image? To prevent embarrassing mistakes, tip 15 percent for lunch. If your party is more than five, tip more. Large groups are harder to serve.

Tip more if you stay awhile. If your service is bad, quietly and quickly call attention to it. If the poor service persists, lower your tip, but leaving none makes you look bad.

You may either leave the tip on the table, at the register, or hand it directly to the server. Tips have been stolen by other patrons, if you can believe it.

Avoid leaving a collection of small coins you dug from your pocket or the bottom of your purse. It looks cheap and unprepared. Of course, you can solve the change problem by using your credit card.

Cultivate a working relationship with a few select restaurants. And tip your regular servers well. Your investment can surely pay off during an important business meal.

There Is More To Being A Guest Than Showing Up At The Party

Being a guest is an art. You know the folks who have been good guests in your life, and you certainly remember those who haven't been.

Being a guest requires a mastery of more subtle behavior than that required for a host. Whether it's for the holiday season or the obligatory cocktail party, you can brush up on your skills with the following tips:

• Honor the hosts. It's simple. Let them know your plans. Respond to their invitation. Let them know if you will be late. If you cannot come, or choose not to come, regret their invitation, but say you appreciate being invited. If at the last minute you cannot attend, call the next day to apologize. Don't develop the reputation of a "no-show."

• If you have not received an invitation to an event you thought you should have, get a third party to inquire for you. Your invitation could have been returned in the mail, or you may not have been included this year. Don't embarrass the host or yourself by asking directly. And bring only the people who were invited, whose names were on the invitation. Don't

Honor the host by attending in the right attire.

assume you can bring extra people.

• Dress appropriately. Honor the host by attending in the right attire. It may take a little research, but find out the tone of the event. You can ask hosts, "What are you wearing?"

• Circulate and mingle. Be ready to introduce yourself to those you don't know. You impose an extra burden on your host when you must be entertained and cannot function on your own.

If you tend to be a little shy, strike up a conversation with someone at the hors d'oeuvres table. Compliment the food or the event and then ask questions such as "How do you know the host?" or "Are you traveling for the holiday?" And realize when you are dominating the conversation.

• Leave before it is time to go. Say you were glad you were included, that you had a nice time. And in the next few days, call or write a note to indicate your appreciation for their work.

Before you start socializing, take an inventory of your skills as a guest. Be aware of your role. You will be appreciated more.

Dos and Don'ts During The Holiday Season

As the holiday season approaches, you have an unusual opportunity to promote yourself with the way you handle business social events. And it may just mean a promotion or the contract you have worked hard for.

At their worst, holiday parties elicit groans from employees and bosses alike for the sense of obligation of expected attendance. Typically, people make their required appearance, say perfunctory hellos, and leave early. Or they get silly and shoot out the chandeliers.

But these parties can provide a real opportunity for being seen in a new light. How you handle yourself at these business festivities indicates you have a broader range of business skills than balancing budgets, organizing committees, and only talking business. Your holiday social skills indicate you know how to be a guest, how to be a host, and simply how to have a good time.

Another opportunity parties provide is to suspend for an evening animosities that have been brewing. Perhaps you can even resolve differences.

Some dos and don'ts to consider during the holiday season:

How you handle yourself at these business festivities indicates you have a broader range of business skills than balancing budgets, organizing committees, and only talking business.

• Do approach the occasion festively. Show people you know how to have a good time, that you can relax, and that you're a human being.

• Do remember this is a business event. Don't be seduced to thinking otherwise. For example, do watch what you drink. Don't get sloppy.

• Do maintain your business persona in your dress, but indicate you have some range. Don't show your lack of judgment by wearing your typical business attire to a cocktail party. Loosen up a bit, but don't dress like a sex idol either.

• Do speak to the bosses and their spouses, to employees at all levels, and be especially attentive to newcomers. So many times, I see people speak only to those they know. Circulate. Mingle. Practice to make your conversation light. And go easy on business subjects.

Professional etiquette at business socials will protect you from making mistakes and may even project you more positively. The strategy is showing you know how to do your work well and have a good time.

Invitations Don't Have To Invite Confusion

So you want to have a big party to tell your customers how much you appreciate their business? Or you want to have your department to your home for a nice evening of fellowship? Perhaps you are one of the lucky ones invited to several events in one evening, some of which you want to attend, some of which you are not so sure.

The way you handle invitations says a lot about your business, and it says a lot about you. With the holiday season in full swing, here are some etiquette guidelines on the art of giving and receiving invitations:

• Make your guests feel special even in the way you invite them. Computer labels and metered postage are about as personal as . . . well . . . who knows? If you are unhappy with your response rate to your RSVP's, look to your invitations as part of the problem. They may be impersonal or uninteresting.

• Be discreet about issuing invitations. Be sensitive to inviting some people and not others, especially if those folks see each other often. You don't have to explain who you are inviting, nor should you broadcast it throughout the office when the office is not invited.

• In receiving invitations, always, always respond to those

Even in this tough old business world, people's feelings get hurt.

requesting an RSVP. Usual response rate is within three days. Those who respond create a considerate and favorable image for themselves.

• Don't brag or name drop that you were invited to LaDeDa event. Even in this tough old business world, people's feelings get hurt. Your boastfulness shows your insensitivity, even shallowness.

• What if you do have conflicts, or you are not sure you even want to go? Call to say you appreciate the invitation, you have some conflicts, but that you'll get back to them by a certain day, if they can wait that long. That can buy you time and foster goodwill. Then make a decision and let them know.

• And what if you were excluded from a guest list? Use a third party to inquire for you. Your invitations could have been lost or returned. But if you were intentionally left off, handle it bravely. Accept your host's decision with good grace. Don't try to finagle one.

• One last tip, let your host know the next day or two, either in writing or by phone, how much you enjoyed yourself. People appreciate those who notice the effort, and that gesture can go a long way in the business world.

Gift-Giving Can Be Inappropriate

Understanding the etiquette of holiday gift-giving for business will enable you to enjoy the process of giving and receiving gifts while protecting your business interests and personal character.

In giving gifts:

• Be frank about the purpose of your gifts. Generally, the purpose influences the selection and delivery, and you want your gesture to be appropriate and in good taste.

Resist giving gifts that may appear to curry favor or create a sense of obligation or that may embarrass you or the recipient. Do give thoughtful gifts to show appreciation or to express goodwill.

• Decide who should receive a gift and who should not. Gifts to bosses are generally unnecessary, but if the group chips in for something, or if a longtime secretary prefers to buy one, gifts to bosses should neither be too expensive nor too personal. A boss may select a small gift or gift certificate for immediate staff or invite them to dinner, but bonuses are not to be considered personal gifts and require only a verbal thanks, not

Resist giving gifts that may appear to curry favor or create a sense of obligation.

a written one.

Gifts are given to fellow professionals and cash tips to people who offer basic services. Personal gifts between peers or coworkers should be exchanged privately.

• In accepting gifts, if a gift is addressed to the company or department, but delivered to the supervisor, it is meant to be shared. If you receive a gift that was well-intentioned, but you question its appropriateness, you may return it with a note saying that you appreciate the gesture, but you are unable to accept the gift and why.

Gifts that are intentionally inappropriate (and it does happen), gifts that are too personal, too expensive, those which imply sexual overtones, or are just a bad joke, may be returned with a note saying only that you are unable to accept the gift. Keep a record of your response to refused gifts in case you are ever suspected of accepting favors.

Ignorance of the protocol of gift-giving in business can hurt you, but being aware of its subtleties can protect the goodwill you want to express.

Gift-Giving Is A Definite Art Form

Spring always brings with it a host of invitations —weddings, graduations, visits — and with the invitations, gifts.

Gifts can be exchanged with bosses, employees, business associates, coworkers, and clients. The exchanging of gifts is an art, especially in business, for it reveals something of a person's character, imagination, thoughtfulness, and generosity.

Those characteristics can be striking in business, especially in contrast with our usual hurried approach to accomplish tasks and satisfy obligations. Because we suspect ulterior motives or are bothered with the perception of bribery, we handle gifts awkwardly and formally. Or, because we are afraid of being misrepresented, we select dull but safe bets, foregoing any flair.

To sharpen your business skills and help you judge gifts appropriately, follow these guidelines:

• Be clear of your purpose. Gifts are given for many reasons and can bring obvious benefits and pleasure. Gifts become

Because we suspect ulterior motives or are bothered with the perception of bribery, we handle gifts awkwardly and formally.

suspect and inappropriate when given to flatter the pride of the giver, secure too obvious an obligation, or satisfy a burdensome indebtedness.

• Consider the timing and presentation. Waiting too long may undervalue the effect. Take care with wrappings. Beautifully presented gifts indicate attention to detail and add to the occasion. Address gifts with thoughtful messages on appropriate gift cards. Notes on business cards may be too impersonal at times.

• Understand how a gift is to be accepted. Notwithstanding wilted bouquets or direct bribes, express appreciation for the thoughtfulness of the giver, even if you cannot accept or don't care for the selection.

Confidence and poise in the giving and receiving of gifts can add to your success as a business person.

Obligatory Thank-You Notes Can Distinguish You

Sincere, original thank-you notes can distinguish you because they have fallen from the habits of "busy" people. Yet, they remain one of those business behaviors you are expected to know.

Here is a brief review:

• Select your stationery carefully. Company logos on smaller fold-over paper, informal cards, and correspondence cards signal a personal message. You also need your own personal selection of blank informals and writing paper designed to suit most occasions and reflect who you are.

• Use ink pens, not ballpoint, and be neat. Handwritten notes are generally favored more than typed, but if you have poor penmanship, or you will otherwise never get around to it, type.

• Select your words carefully. Avoid formal, staid phrases. Put some life into it. Show your appreciation.

• Salutations can begin with "Dear. . :" followed by the way the person prefers to be addressed. Close with "Sincerely." You can err more often by assuming overfamiliarity than by indicat-

Don't dilute your expression of thanks by slipping in requests or discussing other subjects.

ing appropriate deference.

• Lastly, thank-you notes should be just thank-you notes. Don't dilute your expression of thanks by slipping in requests or discussing other subjects.

Write thank-you notes for the following occasions:

—When you receive gifts (within three months for wedding gifts),

—When you have been someone's guest for a meal or been given tickets to an event,

—When you receive personal notes of condolence,

—When you acknowledge a special compliment or show appreciation for a job well done,

—When you interview for a job.

Do not send a thank-you note for a thank-you note. For collective gifts, one thank-you note to the group is appropriate.

Writing thank-you notes well is not done often. Your best effort could make the difference in your being remembered and favored. Besides, it's a basic common courtesy.

Be A Good "Roll" Model

"I hope you don't mind. I have a lot of questions about etiquette," says a tax recruit with Ernst and Young. "For example, at the table, I always wait for someone else to make the first move. I'm tentative in social settings, but I know manners are important for business."

Bill Duncan and Joel Bailey, executives with the firm's National Professional Development Group listened. As part of the firm's two week tax orientation in Vero Beach, Florida, they planned a presentation on the fundamentals of business etiquette with a concentration on table manners.

"We want to give our folks the confidence they need to do their jobs well," says Duncan. "Having appropriate manners allows you to get on with the business at hand. It doesn't impede your ability to work. Bad manners distract. They interfere. It's like chopping rocks with an axe. You damage the tools you need to get the job done. And it's especially important in consulting or management when dealing with people is your business."

With so much work conducted at breakfast or luncheon meetings, here are highlights of the most common table etiquette dos and don'ts:

"Using bad manners is like chopping rocks with an axe. You damage the tools you need to get the job done."

• Begin eating only when most people around you have their plates. If you haven't been served, encourage others to go ahead.
• Avoid waving your eating utensils while you are eating. Business people have been seen jabbing their forks, or worse, their knives at table mates to make a point, and all this while they are still chewing. Don't talk with your mouth full or twirl utensils in the air. And the knife blade goes in, sharp side toward the table edge when placed on the plate between meals.
• Use the bread plate on your left. So often at banquets, people find their bread plate occupied. Don't continue an error. Put your roll on your plate and let the next person have theirs with a tactful, " I believe this one is yours."
• Be conversant. Ever get in a conversation with a one word replier? "How do you like the program?" "Fine." "Been here before?" "No." Make sure the conversation moves around from topic to topic, person to person. No one likes to be left out or cornered.

Take a little time to review table manners. You can be casual at home, but business is more formal. And casual habits don't always reflect well on you or the company you represent.

Home Is Where The Heart Is And Where Entertainment Can Pay Off

Sitting on the porch the other night with friends and family, someone described the fun he had at a backyard party. "Probably a business write-off," he said, "but warm, fun, and easy."

"The hosts were accessible," he added. "Nothing was frantic, and the food was plentiful and tasty. They were masterful hosts."

I could tell from the tone of the conversation that the guests felt honored. Turns out the party was given by one of the most successful small-business executives in the area.

I was reminded of Robert Scarborough, assistant executive director of the S.C. Association of School Administrators, who encourages his members to lobby, and in particular, to lobby members of the General Assembly.

"Anyone can arrange something at a restaurant, and that has its place, but the atmosphere in your home is friendlier, warmer, more personal."

"I tell our members the most effective place to lobby is in your hometown, and the best place in your hometown is in your home."

Scarborough continued, "Anyone can arrange something at a restaurant, and that has its place, but the atmosphere in your home is friendlier, warmer, more personal.

"You get to know people, and they feel comfortable with you. They learn to trust you."

It takes self-assured, organized professionals to have staff, business associates, and even legislators in their homes, but it can connect people on the human terms that make business productive.

Don't talk yourself out of it. It takes practice, but people appreciate the gesture for a long time.

The Right Approach Can Secure A Job

Spring is traditionally job change time. Whether you are a seasoned professional or just entering the job market, you might want to review basic etiquette strategies for a job interview. Too casual or too eager an approach as a candidate may eliminate you, even though your credentials are solid.

• Be prepared. With a little organization, you can win over equally qualified competition. Arrive about 15 minutes early to steady yourself, catch your breath, find the office. Enter five minutes before your appointment. Have plenty of neat résumés within reach, résumés which have been carefully screened for typos.

Rehearse questions you think you will be asked. Stress what you like about the company or the job and how you would fit in. It's so basic, but candidates present themselves as if companies are lucky to have them. Self-confidence can quickly become arrogance.

• Present yourself well. Dress neatly. I hear over and over about how lightly business professionals treat the interview

***It's so basic, but candidates present
themselves as if companies are lucky
to have them. Self-confidence can
quickly become arrogance.***

process. They arrive in casual attire — boat shoes, open neck shirts, jeans, even sweat suits. They smoke, chew gum, put their things on the interviewer's desk, and are rude to the office staff.

The interview is a formal process. Be on your best behavior. Practice your small talk, your handshake, and eye contact. Sit on the edge of your seat.

Let the interviewer begin and end the conversation. You are a guest. Wait to be offered a seat. Unless invited to do otherwise, address the interviewer by "Mr." or "Ms." Thank interviewers for their time and follow-up with a business-like thank-you note. Besides adding a finishing touch, it's just good manners.

Carl Kennedy, 10 years in human resources with Milliken and now supervisor of human resources with Mack Trucks, has noticed how sophisticated candidates have become about the interviewing process.

Yet he adds, "The number one asset, no matter what their field, is the ability to be personable and to work with others."

Beware Of Pitfalls In A New Job

Starting a new job can be tricky whether you just graduated, were promoted and transferred, or hired from the outside to shape up the place. How you approach your new role contributes to your early influence and sustained effectiveness. Here are etiquette tips to ensure your success:

• Be deferential. Know to whom your are accountable. Speak with respect and don't interrupt. Stand (or at least sit up straight) when important people approach.

• Be approachable, easy to meet, and easy to work with. Watch being overly demanding or piously highly principled. You may not have the authority you think you do.

• Determine the office codes of conduct. Listen for how people address one another. In most cases, use titles with

Watch being overly demanding or piously highly principled. You may not have the authority you think you do.

superiors or those older than you, but address everyone with dignity. And be attentive to your business appearance. Yes, the way you dress is important, and good grooming a requirement.

• Expect an adjustment time. Neither be shocked by or revel in cultivating criticism.

• Avoid too much emotional involvement in your work. Being too loyal, too consumed, or too distracted by extreme personalities may prevent you from using the good judgment you were hired for. Take time to refresh yourself. Have other interests.

• Know yourself — who you are and who you aren't. From this will come a quiet confidence that will keep you steady and wise.

The Company Interviewer Has The Responsibility To Recruit

Spring is traditionally interview time, and how companies act as interviewer enables them to recruit the brightest and best. But because of the numbers of talented applicants, interviews often become sloppy. To keep you as precise and professional as you really are, here is a review of the responsibilities of the interviewer:

• Be prepared. It sounds so simple, but too many times interviewer arrogance creeps into the job process. Review the credentials of the candidate before the interview, don't keep the candidate waiting too long, and control interruptions.

Reid Merline, a paralegal who recently joined Nelson, Mullins, Riley and Scarborough, commented about how professional Jean D. Floyd, the paralegal coordinator for the firm, was during the interviewing process. Merline said, "She had reviewed my résumé ahead of time. Instead of asking tricky or vague questions such as 'Tell me about yourself,' she directed her questions to relate my experience with the position she needed filled."

• Present yourself well. You, as interviewer, have a respon-

Being at ease enables candidates to present themselves well.

sibility to present the best image of your company you possibly can. Take care of your own appearance. Sit up straight. Don't kick back casually in your seat just because you have the position to offer. And keep your office neat.

• Work to make the candidates comfortable. Be quick to welcome people. Offer them coffee. Introduce them to nearby coworkers. Being at ease enables candidates to present themselves well, to answer questions that you as interviewer really need to know.

Merline has encountered her share of interviewers who tried to intimidate her. "Interviewers who drilled me with tough questions mistook my quiet response as being scared to voice an opinion, which is certainly wrong."

• Let candidates know where they stand. Don't keep them dangling.

There is no question about it, polished interviewing skills save time and money, motivate staff, and keep employees productive.

Be Yourself In A New Job, But Be Your Best Self

Getting off to a good start is important when beginning a new job. It matters if you were highly recruited or if you competed with hundreds for the job. It matters if you are new to your field or an old pro hired to shake things up. Here are a few techniques to remember as you begin:

• Participate. Join in the activities. Many places of employment have receptions for newcomers. Go. Introduce yourself. Be easy to meet. Don't wait around for others to approach you. If you are shy, introduce yourself to one or two people at a time. Your manner might be quiet, but folks will notice if you are willing to be one of them.

• Treat all employees with equal respect and honor those who should be honored. While it is important to be friendly to everyone, avoid being too friendly too fast. We all notice the gadflies who perk up when the boss is around, who pretend to be tight with the decisionmakers right away, who act bored with everyone else, bark at the administrative staff, and overlook those who keep the building and grounds clean. Just be confident, solid, strong. Honor those in positions of authority with respect, but not gratuitousness.

We all notice the gadflies who pretend to be tight with the decision-makers right away and overlook those who keep the building and grounds clean.

• Take directions willingly. Every employer values someone who respects the requests of supervisors. You may have a better way of approaching a problem, but until you win your new employer's confidence, your suggestions may sound like complaints.

Treva Vinson, a first year math teacher at San Marcos High School in San Marcos, Texas says, "We have some new policies here which are really different from when I was a student teacher. I try to keep my strong opinions to myself. I try to get the feel for the group. I want to wait to see how others handle a problem before I start complaining, and I ask a lot of questions."

• Take inside information about employees in stride. Employees may try to do you favors to warn you off certain projects or people. You can take this under advisement but keep your mind open. Vinson continues, "What people seem to talk about are the people who gossip."

In wanting to do a good job or be noticed, it is easy to be pushy. Take some time to assess your position and the strategies for doing well.

Basic Etiquette Transcends International Borders

Recently, I presented a seminar "International Business Manners" to complement the South Carolina Association of Technical Educators' conference theme, "Technical Education and the Global Challenge." This theme on our role in the international marketplace is becoming more and more pervasive in the workplace. Knowing business customs of other countries reveals insight about our own business culture.

You might enjoy a quick read on international business etiquette. You may find, as I have, that the comparison and contrast of different styles of doing business abroad enables you to conduct your business more effectively, whether you visit another country, host a delegation at home, or find yourself living and working with peoples from cultures different from your own.

Here are a few basic etiquette techniques which transcend international borders, build better business relationships, prevent unnecessary mistakes, and check arrogance:

Knowing business customs of other countries reveals insight about our own business culture.

• Learn the native phrases for greetings, good-byes, and gratefulness. Know how people prefer to be addressed. Here we have a tendency to move quickly to first names, but abroad the process is not as fast. People appreciate brief, general compliments about their country's positive role in civilization, their hospitality, their food. Effusive discourses can be perceived as patronizing and suspect. Be aware of what is considered too personal to ask. It varies. Innocent inquiries can alienate, and there is no use to be unnecessarily insensitive.

• Prepare for your trip or hosting international guests by studying the culture. Approach learning as a basic current events and civics class. Your rudimentary knowledge and sincere interest will build profitable goodwill and prevent you from seeming foolish.

• Avoid bragging about the United States or considering our customs the international standard. We have much to learn from others.

Basic Travel Courtesies Make Good Business Sense

Business trips are unavoidable anymore, and heavy travelers crusade passionately for basic travel courtesies, courtesies which when present make trips go smoothly, and when absent bring out the vengeful wrath of fellow passengers.

Here is a brief review of travel etiquette to benefit even seasoned travelers:

• Have your documents ready. Be friendly at the counters, but businesslike and quick. Flirting with the desk clerks may be fun for you, but can terribly inconvenience someone making a close connection. And that someone may just be at your next meeting.

• Pack manageable luggage. When you find your seat, step out of the aisle so that people can pass. Then put your luggage where it needs to go. Be patient with others who are struggling. Offer to help. And take turns with the aisle seat if you travel often with a partner.

•Respect people's time. Travel may not present the most appropriate opportunity to become someone's pal. People

If a conversation you initiate is met with terseness, take the hint.

work as they travel, relax from hectic schedules, or sleep from exhaustion. If a conversation you initiate is met with terseness, take the hint. To dissuade a talker, either take out your work and get busy, or say, "I'm sorry. I have a lot to do," or "I really need to rest before the next stop." You could add, "Could we visit during the meal?"

• Keep your voices low. Karen Chinn, an associate with Carter Global Associates travels often and says, "My biggest peeves are loud talkers and smokers." She can be sympathetic to a point with traveling groups, "but they get obnoxious pretty quickly."

• Watch what you drink. Travel will dehydrate you, and alcohol takes effect quickly. Before you know it, you'll be sharing trade secrets and company gossip with who knows whom.

Observe the basics of travel etiquette, and you'll arrive at your destination ready for business.

With International Business, Cultural Horizons Need Expansion

Ask a large group of business people if they work internationally, are owned by international businesses, or work with culturally diverse groups, and you'll see a sizable show of hands.

While some cities and businesses already have a long tradition of being international, more and more culturally homogeneous companies and communities are experiencing firsthand the influence of other cultures. And one country that commands our attention is Japan.

Sandra Burleson, president of International Business Communications in Columbia, S.C., helps Japanese and American companies with technical, legal, and business communication training. Here are highlights of what Ms. Burleson finds distinctive about Japanese business practices:

• The Japanese don't take rituals lightly. Even the way business cards are handled is very important, from the way they are presented and received, to having them translated phonetically for correct pronunciation.

• They don't like to be embarrassed, and they consider it rude to mispronounce names. "They are very formal in their

More and more culturally homogeneous companies and communities are experiencing firsthand the influence of other cultures.

introductions, the way they dress, plan and conduct meetings, and address each other with honorifics," she says.

• American traditions of using first names or telling jokes before the meeting to loosen up the group is inappropriate and awkward for Japanese. Even Japanese who have worked with Americans and use first names with Americans revert to the traditional customs of last names with Japanese counterparts.

• Because Japanese don't like surprises, they plan agendas in detail, sending them back and forth, subordinate to subordinate, to have everything in order for the formal meeting.

"They plan itineraries to the minute. And they are long in decision-making," Ms. Burleson says. "The Japanese value consensus because they consider themselves a part of a group, whereas we like to be considered individuals. But once they make a decision, they can execute it quickly. We say we will do it, then figure out how."

By studying the Japanese, we learn three things: how best to do business with Japanese; insight into what we do that is distinctly American; and how we are perceived by others. And all three of these influence our success.

New Products From ETICON For Your Continuing Professional Development

The Audiocassette Program:
 A series of 8 cassette tapes and accompanying handbook that present the most frequent etiquette issues for business settings. This fast-moving, entertaining series includes real life situations we can all relate to, and presents strategies for how to overcome awkward and difficult situations and excel in the face of stiff, honorable competition. Afterall, good business etiquette is not only respected, it's expected.
 Topics are based on the programs Ann offers to business audiences and include:
.... *Creating the Right Impression, Frankly Speaking, Telephone Strategies, Meeting Etiquette, Compliments, Criticism and Apologies, Personal Business Correspondence, Business Appearance, The Most Common Business Etiquette Blunders, Male/Female Protocol, Business Social Events, Human Relations at Work, and A More Powerful You: Self Insight* $89.95

— —

To order, call 1-800-476-4667 or 803-782-4400 or write ETICON, P.O. Box 290116, Columbia, SC 29229-0116 (Tax, shipping and handling to be added. Discounts for multiple copies.

ORDER FORM: Yes! We want to increase our effectiveness!

We want:
 _____**The Right Moves book ($9.95)**
 _____**The Right Moves** cassette ($9.95)
 _____**Book and Cassette**($19.95)
 _____**The Door Swings Both Ways** video ($225 purchase, $100 rental)
 _____Audiocassette Series ($89.95)
 _____Shipping and Handling ($3/package)
$ _____Total Investment

Please print:
Name:_____Title:_____
Address:_____
City:_____State:_____Zip:_____
Phone:_____

Make checks payable to :
**ETICON, P.O. Box 290116, Columbia, SC 29229-0116, or call to order
1-800-476-4667 or 803-782-4400**

About The Author

Ann Chadwell Humphries is founder and owner of ETICON, Etiquette Consultants for Business, based in Columbia, South Carolina. Her business offers speeches, presentations, in-house seminars, and consulting to associations, businesses, professional organizations, and athletes as well.

Her column, "The Right Moves," began in 1988 and is now distributed through Knight Ridder News Tribune wire service to over 250 newspapers nationwide.

Her popular children's program, Camp Manners, teaches 12 lessons on everyday manners to children ages 4-11.

She and her husband, Kirk, live in Columbia with their spirited young sons, Brad and Charlie.